Little Kings

Little Kings

Peter Kahn

Nine
Arches
Press

Little Kings
Peter Kahn

ISBN: 978-1-911027-97-3
eISBN: 978-1-911027-98-0

First published June 2020 by:

Nine Arches Press
Unit 14, Sir Frank Whittle Business Centre,
Great Central Way, Rugby.
CV21 3XH
United Kingdom

www.ninearchespress.com

Nine Arches Press is supported using public funding by Arts Council England.

Supported using public funding by
ARTS COUNCIL
ENGLAND

For Mom, Dad, Grandma Liz, Grandma Grete, Papa Hans, Uncle Al,
Neon Street Center for Youth, Malika's Kitchen & Spoken Word Club.
This book doesn't exist without you.

Contents

I

Grandpa's Fancy Watch

A long, long time ago, before even the iPhone,
Grandpa Hans had a fancy wrist watch.
It had no battery, and nothing to wind it up —
as long as he moved, so did the watch's
hands. It was some slick trick.

Grandpa's forearms looked like holiday
hams. They rippled from the meat
he chopped year after year at the butcher
shop. How did he slip on that watch?

Grandpa would take it off and tell me
to watch the hands slow to a stop.
Don't shoot, they'd say. He'd tell me
to close my eyes and count to twenty.
When I opened them, I'd look at the hands
waving, *We're alive! We're alive!*

The watch died when Grandpa Hans
did, its hands clasped in prayer.

"...Till It's Gone"

A Golden Shovel after Joni Mitchell

When I tell you about Steve, don't
think just because he killed someone, it

means he's a dog to put down. There's always
two sides and while it may well seem

that his story reeks of bug-eyed maggots, to
judge him without the bullet's story is to go

down a light-less dead-end street that
isn't a street after all. When I ask you

to listen for the clink of ricochet, don't
forget to hear the surprise in his voice. Know

he aimed high at stars, not people, to escape what
would be an L platform of snarling fists. You've

no idea what blood and teeth taste like. Got
no idea what it's like when your mom shoots up till

you're sleeping in shit, ripped away by DCFS. It's
like you're riding down a razor. All sense of up, gone.

Little Kings

8th Grade. No parents home at Rob Kenton's house.
Six of us watch *Young Frankenstein* in the basement
buzzed on Little Kings Ale. 8 packs of 8-ouncers.

Green bottles, cuddled like teddy bears we hide
in the closet instead of tossing. Commercial
for *Laverne and Shirley*—we toast the TV. Chuckle

and chug. Stand like chorus girls—kick legs, slur,
5, 6, 7, 8...*schmeil, schmazzle, Hoppenstead
incorporated!* No parents, teachers, bullying big brothers.

The movie comes back on. I-Gor's eyes bulging remind
me of my own, beer-blurred. Parents due in an hour,
we take a last gulp of Little Kings. Each of us vow

to finish off an 8-pack. I stop at five—cautious
then, as now, listening to the retching. Six
had Jeff burping, cursing

his big sister—she bought the beer.
Dr. Franken*steen* calls Frau Blücher and horses neigh
and whinny, kicking their rear legs as we clutch our stomachs.

Seven beers made Rob empty his belly like a torn bag
of groceries. Eight got Karl wide-eyed, muttering snot-filled
gibberish as if the real Frankenstein monster, bolts and all,

was stomping his way. Did he see Rob's pale pieced-together
face waxy from the mortician three years later after riding shotgun
to a drunken Cuervo Gold driver?

The doorbell rings repeatedly—drawing us from
our subterranean castle. Reminding us we were all fuzzy
mustache and puff of bony chest we hoped made us look old

enough to buy our own beer. Three years later, in the funeral parlour
it's clear our crowns were from Burger King. Our kingdom,
youth's puffed up buzz.

Tuesday Mornings at Neon Street Center for Youth

If Steve didn't kill anyone,
it'll be OK. If Steve didn't kill
anyone, it'll be OK. Repeat,

as necessary, before punching
the glowing 4 outside the elevator
at the group home on Sheridan

and Lawrence. A mantra, perhaps
a prayer. Exit on the 4th floor.
Check in with the night staff. Learn

which fears materialised over
your Sunday/Monday weekend.
Who broke curfew. Who ran away.

Who was arrested. Who got kicked
out. Who is new and what ghost
does he carry on his shoulder. Breathe.

White should not be the colour
of your knuckles from the clench.
White should not be the colour of power

and surrender. Of the sheet blooming
a moist rose on the L platform as Steve
runs from gang signs, turned sirens,

turned gun found in alley, turned botched
ballistics, turned funeral and Audy Homes
and Cook County Jail and Statesville. Do not

focus on the number 920—making us
the murder capital. Do not consider 919.
Do not look into the white eyes

of the future or you will hit snooze
until the sun puts itself back to sleep.
Do not let them see the white flag

stutter in your eyes. Do not discuss
guilty until proven innocent. Wake
each kid with a hard knock to the door.

Load them all in the maroon Ronald
McDonald van. Drop them off a block
from their school. Watch them duck

out the van and hear the sliding slam
of the door. Turn off the radio they fought
over, hold tight to the steering wheel

and drive to the drop-in center, alone.

Dear Mrs. Gire

If you hadn't been absent that day,
Mrs. Gire, I would have turned out
differently. With your steel-wire

peppered hair, your curdled-milk skin,
your steely stare, you'd never
have taken us outside in such heat.

Never sat us in a circle on green grass
peppered with pissy dandelions dots.
Asked if we had news to share, like that hippie

sub. Andy Tuzzeo, then best friend
and confidante, would never have dared
to say, *Peter doesn't want school to end.*

He won't be able to see Jill. He likes *her.*
I wouldn't have seen Jill's face
bloom into a stop sign—

eyes darting down, buried
with my eight-year-old ego.
Wouldn't have heard laughter

bombard me like red rubber balls in gym.
If you weren't absent that sunny day,
Mrs. Gire, confidence wouldn't have

stunted like a plastic stump.
Asking Megan Mott to senior prom nine
years later wouldn't have sent me

to the emergency room: nose bleeding out,
turning white tissue to gloppy sludge.
Were you truly sick that day, Mrs. Gire?

I really hope so.

Waiting with No Vocabulary

Neither of us speak
Spanish, other than to say,

No hablo Espanol and
we're in Barcelona, which

in Spain, we learn, is pronounced
BarTHElona and it's 1988

and there's no Google translate,
no Google anything,

and *Let's Go Spain* is a book that can't
answer *What do you do*

when your girlfriend is screeching
in pain that sounds like a burst

appendix and no one understands
English and you're thinking

of what you'll say (in English)
to her parents who will have

to transport her body back
to Boston? There *is* a phone

number in *Let's Go* for a British
hospital and you convince

the front desk at your cheap
hotel to let you use their rotary

phone or your girlfriend will die
in their cheap, flimsy bed.

And soon you play charades
with the ambulance driver

who eventually helps you
carry your possibly dying girlfriend,

like an over-sized suitcase,
or, let's face it, a casket,

down four flights of creaky stairs,
but you can't charade your way

into going to the hospital with them.
So you sit in a spring-shot chair

waiting and waiting with no
vocabulary for what might happen,

with no one and no way and no hablo.

2771

You are a number and a home. A place
that made me, with a neighbour who deflated
me like the basketball that stammered
into her front yard to die alone, the electric
fence that wasn't there keeping me
with you, 2771. Mrs. Lancia was a ghost
that haunted long before she died
and somehow she's there each time
I visit you, bullying from across the way,
undaunted by the zinnias Mom planted
to pretty the view.

On top of the Monte Carlo

in North Miami Beach, almost thirty floors up,
there's an Orthodox Jew smoking a cigarette and gasping
at the ocean. I do that too sometimes, wondering if

the waves think they can catch up to one another.
I am jogging and dodging feral cats who weren't here
a few years ago, but dart about like water-less minnows

across this path, and I wonder if this smoking Jew is
from Paris. There are lots of French-speakers down
here and their words swim into my ears soaked

with Yiddish I don't understand but understand.
And I am a Reform Jew, if that, and I don't smoke,
but I am running and thinking of Grandpa who smoked

a pipe and how he was Orthodox for a while in NY,
but he never talked to me about that, nor about much
of anything from his past. He spoke German until

he fled the Gestapo on some rickety ship to Brazil
where he learned Portuguese and made it
to the States and learned English and how to be

an American citizen—he did tell me about that.
I speak un peu du Francais, the "pretty" language
Grandpa told me to study instead of the ugly claw

of German, but can't imagine having to flee my home,
my country, my language for simply being what I was
born to be and I am agnostic and believe God shakes

his head like Grandpa used to while He watches religion
puff and puff and blow too much down. And there was
Bullay's mayor telling Oma to sell everything for something

or get nothing at all. Either way, she had to leave.
And Oma took everything she could fit in a suitcase
rather than take anything Nazi. And she ended

up in New York and her mom ended in Theresienstadt
or Auschwitz, we'll never know. And as I double back
past the Monte Carlo I look up to see if the French Jew

is still there, but I can't even see remnants of smoke
testifying he even existed. Was he there at all?
Was He? And I think of how there are no more

Kahns living in Germany. *Puff*—some mirrors
and smoke trick—and I wonder what my Grandfather
would or wouldn't say in between puffs of his pipe,

at what it's like to be a Jew in Paris or one standing
alone on the roof of a hotel in Miami Beach
as clouds slow-march over waves that billow

and billow towards some kind of safe shore.

An Evening Prayer

After the stunned skunk unleashed
his mighty cologne, Uncle Al bathed old Caesar
in can after can of tomato juice. I remember
his whining barks, tail hanging like a headless

cobra. How Uncle Al chanted a Hebrew lullaby
trying to get a wag out of him.
The next Thanksgiving, the diarrhoea
dripping the length of Caesar's tail, brown-

inking the carpet. The corner whispers of Mom
and Aunt Sheila. The putting down. The red
daze of Uncle Al's eyes. Our faces, bowed
and silent, during dinner. My sneaked look up.

They say Alzheimer's patients recall smells
even when words are swallowed too deeply
to be voiced. May Uncle Al lose his sense
of smell before the rest of him sloughs away.

Time Machine

I was so rich, I shredded thousand dollar bills
over my caviar and gold-flake salad. Sprinkled
diamond dots on top for extra texture. Brought
the Redwood Forest from California to my back
yard for extra privacy. The sun has to knock
for permission to enter. The moon diddies.
So rich, I bought a limo for my limo. A house
for my house. So rich, Beyoncé left Jay-Z
for me. I paid him to write a love song for her
to croon to me. (It was lovely.) So rich,
I had Steve Jobs' ghost Apple me a time
machine. I went back to White Plains
hospital where Grandma Liz lay
alone. 1984. Whispered goodbye for her final
twenty days, grasping her branch of a hand
until her last sigh crawled into the stars' blinking eyes.

The Rake

When Audrey and her big sister, who once wore me
like a backpack as I tried to keep her from killing

another kid, when Audrey and her sister launch
out of the Ronald McDonald's van and flood rush-

hour traffic on Sheridan Road, I know I am not enough.
They swing the shovels and rakes they were paid

$4.25 an hour to put to better use, at the boys
who woof *whore* at them until blood and busted

brake lights stoplight the street. I have no words
for the police, just deep breaths, open palms

and droopy shoulders. They shove me back with,
What kind of caseworker are you anyway?

I want to tell them I am a 22-year-old surrogate
parent with twelve kids, that I wake them

for school every morning and get cursed out
for it, that the principal calls me to fetch them

each week when they're suspended. That
my throat's sore from heart-spit speeches

that bring a roll of eyes and suck of teeth.
That I bring my kids to the emergency room

and sit for hours for their stitches, which get ripped
out half the time for a return trip. That Neon Street

Center for Youth, meant for homeless teens and wards
of the state, is my second home. That the guards

at the Audy Home detention center know me by name
and the judges shake their heads when they see me again.

After a month in the Audy Home, Audrey and her sister return
to Neon Street for a black-eyed week. When their cousin,
just thirteen, beats a boy's teeth out at school, because

she could, I'm limping towards a stint in grad school.
When she knots a knife into the stunned skull of the girl
stupid enough to try to rob the Air Jordans off her

daughter's four-month-old feet, I know I'm just not
big enough to care so much, and do so little. The *I'll stay
with you for a month or two and then get my own place*

I promise cousin Mike has turned into nearly two years
plopped on his futon couch. The $19,200 a year salary
means I'm eating donated lunches at the drop-in center

with the kids, and Ramen noodles or $1.50 tacos for dinner.
My stomach churning against me each night in a battle
that's killing my sleep and bagging my eyes blue.

Another caseworker, when she hears the white flag
in my voice, tells me to think of my time at Neon Street
in dog years. I make it to double-digits and flee for a human life.

How Do We Make It a Building?

Too many students are half-whole
or a quarter-whole or a dug hole.
And who holds the shovel?

And how do we make it a building
tool? And how can it fill the very hole
it dug without burying anyone?

Too many students are shovels.
In the slipped grip of calloused hands.

Driving to the Cemetery

As Dad and I drive to the cemetery,
I ask about my grandparents, who
we are going to visit in tombs,
entombed too high to touch, 'buried'
ten feet above ground alongside
my great aunts and uncles.

Uncle Erie, the youngest brother,
who made it to 94, when he was
the oldest by default, couldn't sleep
envisioning worms and maggots
ploughing the field of his body
and Grandpa, who had been
the oldest and made it one month
short of 89, wasn't one to rock
the boat (side note: Grandpa
was the first to flee Germany
on a big boat to Brazil), so Grandpa
gave in to be buried in a tomb,
to keep close to his brothers
who he last left in 1935, when
he was still young and still
the oldest.

Dad and I arrive with stones
to show we had been there
and place them one by one
under each name—all that's
left of three brothers, along with
the stories we keep telling
and telling like a boat floating
to a new life.

What Made You Fall...

It wasn't when your teeth tapped, like a spoon against an egg, when she first let
you kiss her. Nor when you first fell into bed together like you were drunk,
when you weren't. Not when she told you she went on the pill. Nor
when she vice-gripped you when you tried to get out of her bed
to go back to your apartment. Not even when she told you
she thought she was falling in love with you and
eight hours later you whispered, Me, too. It was
when she asked you to put in her contact lens.
She held open her right eye. You cradled
her face in your left hand and carefully
did it, watching a single tear
slow-kiss its way down
her cheek.

"...Recipe for Me"

A Golden Shovel after K-OS

Ask me about the sun in summer, when I've
bathed in her trance, danced in her hot flash, been
with her deep into the London night, when even off is on.

When alarm clocks rust in dusty, dank drawers with the
thick thermal underwear I'll yank out for a December run.
Ask me about the sun when my bones are oiled. When this

poem's blurred with sweat. When I'll cast a robust shadow
that waves backwards, grins ahead. When time weighs
helium. Not the dead dark lead that buries me like a

worthless lump of treasure under flannel covers. A ton
of wool laid on top like a blanket of soil and twigs. I
fight winter like a cold that snorts snot with a know-

-ing smile. I'm armed with a dead solar battery I
heaved in the snow. It'll turn up in the lost-and-found
come June. I wish I were lost deep in a warm warp the

whole way through. That Grandma Liz could whisper the recipe
for her mythic Matzah ball soup. I'll taste its warm weight for
as long as the sun fights to get up. I need that uppercut in me.

Skull-and-Bones

"[24 year old] Marlins pitcher Jose Fernandez had cocaine in his system and was legally drunk when he was killed in a boating accident last month, according to autopsy and toxicology reports obtained by ESPN on Saturday."
– ESPN.com, Oct. 30, 2016

Grandma Liz is gone thirty-three years, Grandma Grete is gone
twenty-seven years, Grandpa Hans is gone twenty years. Papa
Lou was gone before his memory could etch itself in me. I miss him. Amen.

Eric's gone twenty-three years. He'd be about forty had gangs not
chosen Lakeview High's courtyard for an after-school us-versus-them
wrong-place-wrong-time skull-and-bones display of daytime fireworks. Amen.

Ishma's gone eight years. She wouldn't even be thirty had the bullets
stayed cosy in the gun. If the gun hadn't been bought dirty in an alley.
If the gun hadn't been made a right per the cocky Constitution. Amen.

My freshman year roommate Adam is gone at forty-nine, chemotherapy
toothless. My ex brother-in-law gone at fifty-two, chemotherapy a bald-faced lie.
My Uncle Chuck is seventy-six. May chemotherapy get him to seventy-seven. Amen.

Some poison's not potent enough. Some poison's our own creation. Some poison's
one man's high and another's casket. Be gone, drugs. Be gone, guns. Be gone,
cancer, no matter its ubiquitous form. Amen. Amen. Amen.

II

Quit

Funk Finecast Factory. Columbus, Ohio. Fall, 1984.

Not the sooty sludge of snot
that blew from my nose each night
when I drilled math equations into my head.

Not the smirking crooked-armed clock
stunning time like a thick truncheon,
clubbing each minute to sleep.

Not even my boss and his "come to Jesus"
coercions resurrected each $3.35-an-hour
day tattooing my ten-minute breaks.

It was burly and bearded *Bear*. The swastika
etched on his left arm. Staring at me
with each drop and dig of the dull-headed drill.

Wolf Man of Wicker Park

People used to shit themselves,
Wolf Man tells me, *when they'd see me.*
I try to picture the growl

of his swagger back when
slack-skinned prostitutes used
to chew the edges of these streets.

When pitchforks and five-pointed stars
decorated cheap siding, claimed
territory like dog piss on trees.

I see the howl in his eyes'
dulled edges when stories
of beat-downs and drive-bys

creep through his oversized teeth.
Halloween of '98 he says, *Rat-ta*
tat tat — seven, eight times.

He tugs up the side of his shirt
to show the gut scars like tiny
stars and one full moon. Putting

down his bottle of Magnum, he excuses
himself to do what one does when
the colostomy bag has reached its sludgy fill.

"Something About..."

a left-handed Golden Shovel after John Murillo

Something tilts like a star standing
on its hip. It's not
about the drift of her eyes.
The smoke of her smile.
A surge twinkling the water
that 90-percents you. It's the
hiss of waves slapping sand, the heat
of her skin. The future
lurking with a long, healthy shadow.
The hum of breath
between breaths when you wake
up next to her sleeping,
notes spilling like water edging
its way over a tin roof's lip.

Turn

They cancelled the first game of the season
right before the fifth inning, the pitch turning
Todd's eye swollen and black. Purple really.
That summer a blue jay picked on a red cardinal
in my back yard, a carpet of crab apples.
I would wake up extra early to beat Dad and get
the fresh-faced paper to read the Reds' box score.
That September, we'd usually go to Todd's house
after school, though I heard my Mom say Todd's mom
was "a little strange." Todd's mom always gave us candy
like Halloween was a family holiday they celebrated
every day. Mom gave us cut up apples that turned brown.
The last time Todd was over, we played whiffle ball
in the backyard. Mom called us in to watch the TV —
Nixon's eviction after turning the White House grey.
This is history, she whispered to us, eyes welling,
before we shot back outside to finish the game.
That Tuesday, Mom wanted me to come straight
home — she was taking me to get a fresh pair
of Buster Browns — so Todd and Kevin forked right
while I traversed the ravine towards the dead end.
Later Kevin told me that Todd's mom told him
to go home when Todd went in. Todd ran out
screaming and his mom screamed, *Get back*
in here! and he did. Kevin stumbled home alone.
The next morning Todd became a story
I wasn't allowed to read in the *Columbus Dispatch,*
the paper missing from the front porch. Todd's dad
that morning, Todd after school, and Todd's mom
as sirens approached, turning the gun on herself.
I came in from the empty porch, my parents there
pajama-ed, eyes shuffling and stuttering like zombies.

In voices I'd not heard before, they told me
that they would always love me, they'd never
hurt me even though Todd's mom, who I thought
loved Todd—didn't all mothers love their kids?—turned
crazy, putting a red end to their family.
I couldn't sleep, one eye open, seeing a howl
in my mother's eyes, grey starting to invade
the black flow of her hair, afraid she might turn, too.

Fire-Forgotten

After "Ghosts" by Anne Sexton

Some WWI ghosts wear Iron Crosses,
no longer hero, nor fully vermin—
their yellow stars, bright as Zyclon B.
Not German Jews, but ghosts
who still claim Germany, lolling their bloated tongues
like turbined Swastikas.

Not all ghosts are Nazis.
I have heard others—
shrunken, snap-backed grandmothers
wearing ashes like fire-forgotten logs.
Not one in six million, but ghosts.
This one shrieks rip-throated, creaking
under my bed.

Some ghosts are babies.
Not weening, but ghosts,
flopping like wounded ducks
on any skyline, or dropping,
losing their empty chances, gurgling
for ghost-eyed parents.

Upstairs at Ronny's Steakhouse

Circa, 1992.

Hey white boy! This ain't
American Bandstand! This is the Soul
Train! Now move them hips! shoots
out of some stranger's mouth
after a woman, winking, pulls me
pre-rum to the naked wooden square.
It's usually packed already
but it's the first time upstairs
has been open since the cops
closed it down three months earlier.
My crew falls out of the booth
as I rickety-rock my hips to
The Percolater, looking like a rusty
pendulum, even though I'm only
twenty-four. Joyce buys me a double
that floor-burns the back of my throat.

I remember one Friday when Joyce and I
bottom-up at least six times before I step
onto that squared-square in front of the DJ
booth. Bobby busts a broken Butterfly
with a light-skinned woman
seven inches taller and one-hundred
jiggly pounds heavier than him.
Reba's hips pendulum against a grinning
old guy who feigns fainting in her arms.
It's time for the percolator, It's time
for the percolator, gyrates the air: the amp's hot
breath blasting our soaked bodies as we bump
and dip and grind into one heap of happy
hour in the Loop of the most segregated
city in America, where I'm the only white
person each week, a true stereotype stumbling
around looking drunker than I could ever be.

Independence

We got to Tremont Park early that first time.
Laid out a checkered blanket, waited and watched.
Lara and I stickied our small hands with red,
white and blue popsicles. As the sky blackened
and white-headed zits twinkled and winked,
there was a quick pop, like a pinned balloon.

Then came the clap that shook my stomach
like a hard hiccup. I loved the colour tie-dying
the dark, but the sound, the way it smacked
the ground, made me cringe and cry and kick
over the bottle of Barolo my parents
were drinking to toast our 199th birthday.

We were the first to leave, retreating to our white
Chevy station wagon. On the drive home, Dad
taught me a game—to clap in sync with each boom,
to ready me for the big 200 when I would be ten,
too old to run from what explodes in the dark.

Sweating Through My Suit

Taped to the off-white wall (beside the bed, yes
her/our bed) of the room where she lived
and I visited before I moved to where we were
both to live (and I still do and she never did)
is a black and white strip of four little photos
of us smiling at the future. The photo booth
stood outside at wedding party and I was sweating
through my suit. She smiled, "This will be us soon enough."

White is the noise black-holing my chest.
White is the shadow between the black slashes
on a clock's forced face. White is what's left
when embers blacken cold. White are the borders
on the photo strip with the black moons
of our pupils gazing from the white heat
of the geyser of a flame between us. Look closely
you can still feel the ~~cackle~~ crackle of it.

Two years later I put all photos of us in a metal
bowl, set them alight, and doused their embers
with cold water in the kitchen sink. Last summer,
I am told, she did get married. I can still picture
that photo strip (torn from the wall and ripped
to bits?), but now see the white of her dress,
a wedding I wasn't suited for.

Elmer's Glue Girl

I picture Mrs. Gire grabbing
that bottle from your 2nd grade fingers.
Fist wagging in your face as she catches
you chomping the rubbery white eyeballs
you rolled off your hairless arms after
warning you again and again, *That will
make you sick*! I couldn't stop munching
malted milk balls, even though they gave me
tummy aches, so I didn't see the difference.
Still, what made you even think to turn glue
into your candy? It was like you were
under a spell. I think Mrs. Gire
was trying to teach you a lesson
that day when she said, *Go ahead. Eat
as many as you want*. You squeezed
the bottle and squirted a trail up your arm.
You were like a proud cake maker creating
your icing design. You knew just when it
had dried enough to make your special
white treats. We watched like it was
one of those little movies Mrs. Gire
showed to teach us about spelling.
We heard the blurp and saw viscous
vomit oozing from your mouth, spilling
white lava onto Mrs. Gire's stiff black shoes.
Jill following suit from the stench. Then Kevin,
Todd and Andy. Me, running like a flash
of camera, fingers stuck in nostrils
hearing the gurgled splash you created
without crayons or round-tipped scissors.
Mrs. Gire rang her bell and one by one,
we came back into the room. She wiped
off her shoes and yelled at us without
looking up. We couldn't find you.

Do you remember the quiet of me?
Was I nice to you, like I remember
or did you see my sprint as abandonment?
I'm a teacher myself and I'm afraid
I'm becoming stiff like Mrs. Gire.
I try teaching lessons and think
of you when they fail. Can you
see what she was trying to do, letting
you eat yourself sick? We never saw you
again. It's like the glue glopped you
from the inside, gooed you translucent.

How It Was Then

That's how it was then, Matzah
balls sinking or floating depending
on which grandma rolled them.
Nana Liz's puffy fluffs; Nana Grete's

dense zeppelins. Well after they were each
gone from us, Lilo—Uncle Walter's late-in-life
girlfriend—invited me over each month
to her 8th floor apartment overlooking

Lake Michigan's rolling waves. She'd make
them more like Nana Liz and it felt
right to watch them float before taking
a spoon to them. Lilo's twist was a pinch

of parsley she'd snap over the soup
like a magician. When she finally had to
give in to the weight of her late eighties
and give up her independence, she

moved to a retirement home, still
on the lake, but way too far up north.
I never managed to make it there.
We met up once at a Jewish deli, halfway

between, but it felt like cheating—
the soup weepy and heavy with salt.
When Lilo stopped returning my calls,
my message after message, the reality

rolled and rolled in my head till finally
I got the call from her nephew,
who told me little but to say I wasn't
in her will. He didn't understand

all I ever wanted was the magic
of a grandmother. Wouldn't
we all try for that if we could?

Verboten

Grandma and Grandpa were done
with Germany in the mid-thirties.
They knew it was time to leave.
Got out just in time and never
went back. Grandma would have,
but Grandpa said it was verboten.

***

The 'right to return' got me a German
passport so I could live in London.
Grandma and Grandpa were done
on this earth so I asked my great
uncle what Grandpa would have thought.
Use them like they used us. Not everyone
in the family knew the right time to leave.

***

I miss hearing my grandparents speak
in German, even though they never
taught me more than wasser, auf wiedersehen,
or guten morgen. While it wasn't verboten,
Grandpa seems to be saying, *We* had *to
learn English, but you don't need German.*

***

I hate the German accent like it was a swastika
spitting in my ears. Like it was a Gestapo
guard igniting the oven. Like it was Hitler's
hideous half moustache. His stiff salute.

***

Dad just unearthed Grandma and Grandpa's
German passports. There's a swastika stamped
on each, like a tattoo stamped on a baby's face.
A going away gift. A don't come back gift.
An open-oven-door-if-you-dare-return gift.

***

Grandpa told me he had been German first,
Jewish third. There was no second. German
first, not Jewish. His father earned the Iron
Cross fighting and dying for his country. German.

***

Once, I got a cheap flight from London to Rome.
We had to change planes in Munich. *No
sprechen sie Deutsch,* I practice on the stiff line
to the German customs agent. I hand over
the green Deutsch-pass with a *Guten Tag.*
He blasts me with questions in German. *No sprechen
sie Deutsch.* More clipped German, then:
*How do you have a German passport and not
speak German? I've got two passports—I'm American.
Hand me your American passport.* He disappears
holding both of my worlds in his German hands.

***

There's a swastika stamped on my Grandparents'
passports. A parting gift. Had they stayed
they would have joined the rest of the family:
yellow-starred, smash-glassed, force-laboured,
huddled, piled, ashed to ash.

***

What's our equivalent? Will they craft
wooden MAGA stamps with wet pads of blood-
ink for our border? Will they tattoo numbers
on arms? Or faces? When will we know
it's time to leave?

"Grayed In and Gray..."

a Golden Shovel after Gwendolyn Brooks

We crave the comfort of colour, like leaves, like skin, like dirt. We
flutter our eyes, hankering for change's constant wheel. We are

the spin & rasp, the spokes & blur, the smoke & bellow. The things
hanging quietly in the garage. Hiding deep in the attic. What of

us? The coats, lost? What of the moments drowned in dust, dry
with creaking veins, cracked? Days languid & limp, leaking hours

like maple syrup-ing silently from decapitated trees? Months and
years tip-toeing, joining their marrow-tapped hands until the

decades bleed soot & ash, and loam begins its involuntary
freeze. What of those appled August afternoons we play-

ed in the backyard, the dog bounding about before his grayed
hide was put to sleep? Before tears dripped like November leaves in

piles you cannon-balled into with your little sister choking on giggles and
emerging red & yellowed long before the night of your hair ash-ed gray.

On Seventeen Years of Teaching

Forget Shanece, the slice on her wrist, purple and puffy.
Forget Wendy, her 33-year-old man-friend, the bloody pregnancy.

Forget Efrom, the sleepless batter of night, its repeat.
Forget Deebo, his heart, the attack that crept and sneaked.

Forget Denise, the *fuck you* grenade she had to release.
Forget Elise, how heroin's leash yanked her to her knees.

Forget Therese, the alley men, how her gagging mouth appeased.
Forget every stricken student, if you can. Every and each atrocity.

Pretending Not to Notice

I talk to the cards—Mantle, Snider and Mays—wanting
to hear about the New York of my father's childhood,
when Grandpa wouldn't close the butcher shop on Saturdays

even when the Dodgers played the Yankees. *Duke, did you
know Dad ditched school once, snuck into Ebbets Field,
to see you play?* He couldn't sit down for a week

after Grandpa found out. I am eight or nine and Dad is
in China or Brazil for business and Grandpa is
in Florida playing gin and I am in Ohio eavesdropping

as Mrs. Durant tells Mom about what Mr. Durant packed
and what he left foul-balling the house: his father's purple
heart pinched in her palm, the reason he'll surely be back.

I have Mickey, Duke and Willie laid out carefully on my desk waiting
for me while I catch glimpses of Mrs. Durant's closed fist and the blood
dribbling down into her lap with Mom pretending not to notice.

The Iron Cross is all that's left of my great-grandfather.
WWI: a wound leading to a bed, welcoming pneumonia,
coughing fatherlessness on my Grandpa and his two brothers.

It's Grandpa's brother Ernie who tells me how
Grandpa wouldn't get out of bed for weeks
after his best friend sewed on a swastika and ceased

talking to him after 23 years as friends. Grandpa wouldn't speak
of it. But I am nine and I haven't heard that story yet,
nor held the Iron Cross that meant bravery and now dregs ash.

"Sitting Here In..."

A left-handed Golden Shovel after Jimmy Cliff

Sitting perched on a leaf-less branch, there is a crow croaking
here and there, waiting for his lover. The offbeat song fades

in and out for hours before you feel the sick symbolism of his
limbo lurch in your throat's lump. Maybe she's already in Florida

knowing he's still waiting to flee together. Maybe she knows
that he'll wait till snow buries his beat-less wings. Maybe she thinks,

"I am not ready to nestle down." Maybe she's met a winking hawk and they
have been making eggs. Regardless, you know if this continues, you'll have

to unearth a baseball from the black back of your closet's clutter,
go to the street's curb and put an end to this throaty hitch of blues.

Pavlov in Chicago

"Some dogs don't bark anymore at the sound of gunfire
in Chicago's Lawndale neighbourhood."
  — *The Chicago Tribune*, July 1, 2012

What would Pavlov make of this? What
have we become where funerals are the new
Bar Mitzvah, baptism, birthday party

for 13-year-olds in Lawndale? My former student
Kyndall's cousin dead at thirteen. Straight A's
and scholarship casketed a day after 8th grade graduation.

Kyndall mutters his murder like it's a commencement
march, not a funeral. Dead-eyed, and tearless,
she tells me about it like a heat wave, a movie,

a breaking up. She draws closer, whispers,
"He was a great kid, but he was in a gang. Everyone
there is." And when will the dogs stop wagging

their tails? When will they stop barking no matter
the blasting ring? Do they know we've given up
before we do?

Loathe

To love
or
to loathe:
they both
begin
and end
the same
way.

The Surprise of It

The sun, that tricky polished coin, plays a game
with Mom's eyes as she edges us onto
Riverside Drive for the ten-thousandth time.
A woman in a car I don't remember slapshots

our Chevy till it's a crumpled shell.
Can you feel the skid and scud of it?
The punch and thud of it? Can you hear the whir
of ambulance and its zooming halt? See

Mom's thumbs up as she's stretchered in.
In the end, only our once-white station wagon
has any permanent injuries. If airbags had existed,
their deflated corpses would have testified

to the crash. Our car looked like a discarded
candy wrapper, but I walked up the hill with not
even a limp. You wouldn't think it possible.
Our neighbour Mrs. Durant, who heard the bash

and bang, even with the buffer of storm window,
chaperoned me to my house. All we could
think to do was turn on the TV to distract me
from the rewind and replay of my brain.

We watched the Soviets take a puck to the teeth
and America win the gold. If you read the sports section
that morning, you knew it was impossible, but we saw
with our own eyes. For a couple of hours, I forgot

about Mom, which too seems impossible. When
the match ended and the crowd stormed the ice,
I slobbered onto Mrs. Durant's fluffy sweater
at the odds of it, the surprise of it, the accident of it.

In 1979, the Shah of Iran is deposed

And Shirami is not eight and a half hours ahead
in Tehran, but here at noon in Columbus
in the locker room at Hastings Junior High
where week after week Brad Kern makes
him cry. And for week after week my friends
and I let the brass knuckles of Brad's words
sucker-punch Shirami and we revel when
the first tear takes the one-way trip down
his cheek, followed by snot and sobs
and unlike my friends I *do* look down,
though I don't want them to know
that I don't want to be at this "Welcome
to America" party. And now I am five
hours ahead here at the Poetry School
in London as I lead this time-travelling
workshop and conjure up the sock-stunk locker
room where on this particular afternoon
Brad Kern gives Shirami a wedgie, yanking
and yanking until the Grandma Liz in me
finally stands up straight and I tell Brad,
loud enough to punch through the laughter, *Enough*
is enough. And the bully in Brad doesn't know
what to do but busted-grin and slow walk-out
of the stench. And Shirami shudders and shakes
and I stay until stillness sets in and we slowly
walk to Geometry class where Mrs. Smith blinks
with a stunned stare as the door opens during
her lecture and for the first time in 7th grade,
I'm late.

Mrs. Lancia

I never left the house without checking
to see if you were out there. Bending
over every school morning

to pick up the *Dispatch* from your porch
flashing elephantine piss-yellow panties
unable to conceal your flabby trunk.

Remember the time you tried
to run Mom over, somersaulting
her into the grass? The time

you knocked our mailbox down
and made drunk cackling threats?
How you'd wake us with a beeping *Why*

are you in bed and not in church?
Remember the morning Dad banged
on your hood trying to scare the honk

out of you? Do you remember
the 10-year-old me mowing the front
lawn, you lounging on a plastic chair

gaping me like I was a six-legged dog
ripping up your lawn? Like I was a black-
hatted Jew polluting your Aryan view.

I'm sure the police muttered, *Not again,*
when their radios belched out your address.
My friends wanted to burn a pile

of shit on your doorstep, wanted to egg
the face of your house, blast your rust
buckets with baseball bats, wanted to crank-

call you with death threats until you
wanted to move off of Lakinhurst Drive. I hated
you, was scared shitless of you, but I always

said no, hearing Grandma Liz and her
Treat people how you want to be treated.
I'm a teacher now, Mrs. Lancia,

about the age you were when we moved
in across the street. One day I asked
my students to write about a crazy neighbour.

Told them about you, how I wished
you dead. One student, tougher than most,
gasped and said, *That's wrong, Mr. K.*

It made me remember you held hostage
to your grey, one-story house after
your runty dog had choked on its barks,

your defeated husband had been casketed,
your scowling daughters had moved off,
and blocked your calls like our dead-end.

That's wrong, Mr. K. It made me
remember you pale and skinny
-ed by age. Time, more ruthless than me.

"...Shooting at Nothing Here"

A Golden Shovel after Jim James

How's a test aim to measure our teaching when a kid's smoking
pot every battered morning before school to muzzle himself from
bubbling a No. 2 pencil into his dad's cross eye. From shooting

a smudged *fuck you* from the ridged barrel of his throat. Look at
it through the daze of his red-marked pupils. Nothing
in a test booklet musters an answer to fasten his focus here.

III

Just Missed

Moving furniture, out flutters
a letter with Slinky-ed scribble
addressed to *Liz Paley,*
Edgemont, NY 10583.

I remember licking the stale
salve of the envelope before
dropping it into the mail box's
blue mouth. Watching it

gulped down into its squared
belly outside Big Bear, with
the Buckeye leaves glued
all over the window. Remember

wondering when it would plop
through the half-grin slot
at Grandma's apartment.
Picturing her veiny hands

grasping for the silver
opener and slicing through
what I had close-kissed
shut.

It was after the funeral, when
we pushed open the door to her apartment,
heard it cough on the mail clogging
the floor, that I realised it arrived a day

or two too late. The *hope*
you feel better drifting
unread into the gaping mouth.

I put the envelope, now looking its age,
behind the hanging wire
at the back of a little abstract
painting Grandma Liz made

for me. Every few years, I look at the script
that's mine, but barely anymore.
Last year, the envelope opened
its lips but I won't read what I wrote:
that's for Grandma's eyes only.

On First Knowing You're a Teacher

Robert's not coming in my boss tells me.
I'm sitting sweating in a windowless office,
a stack of resumes eye-balling me, stinking
up the desk—I'm first screener and sleepy
in this stuffy box. *Would you be able to lead
a workshop on resume writing?* I'm 22
and my own resume got me the most boring
gig at Jobs for Youth-Chicago. Some of the 'youth'
I'd be teaching are nearly my age, but there are
windows, and people, in that classroom
so I nearly yell, *yes!* 30 students look at me
and 45 minutes later look *to* me and I'm hooked.
And I'm floating and anchored at the same time.
For the first time. And I'm whole and broken
open. And I'm spinning and stunned still.

All I Hear is Kaddish

My uncle is squeezing a dog's chew toy,
squeaking the peep out of it, as we walk in,
my parents and me, to this home that is not
where my cousins grew up, but where elders
grow down. My uncle is standing, his head
yanked by gravity like he's looking for a dropped
key or a secret exit or a buried treasure.
A cantor, Uncle Al married my parents,
he married my cousins, married my sister,
married my best friend and hundreds of others.
He would have married me if I got that far.

I choose to join my parents for this visit
to the Alzheimer's Home, instead of catching
a matinee, or reading in Central Park, or doing
shots of rum to celebrate spring break. Anything
to avoid seeing the not-him of him. But I'm here
and Uncle Al sobs at the sight of us.
My Mom shakes at his sobbing. I want him to sing
like he used to, making Caesar howl
or me giggle, but all I hear is a Kaddish
for what's gone and the funeral that will come.
How does it come to this? A brain sponging
memory away like slop. After he stops crying, it hits:
he must know who we are. We're still in there.

But an hour later, as the aide reads *Treasure Island*
aloud, like my uncle is a four-year-old, I'm ready
to leave this sinking ship of a place.

Fifteen men on the dead man's chest—
Yo-ho-ho, and a bottle of rum!
Drink and the devil had done for the rest—
Yo-ho-ho, and a bottle of rum!

Uncle Al parrots back, *I love you* as we back away.
It's hard to know how to feel. It's like coming home
to piss and shit and the wagging tail of the dog
you dreamed had run away.

The Sombre Room

I'm in the home of her parents
who will become my in-laws

if all tilts sunny for this full
family meet-and-greet.

Dinner is a stroll down the aisle,
warm chicken over rice, green peas,

smiles and nods and a tuxedo-d future.
I see relief sun-rising in her eyes.

Her brother, her sisters, even her parents—
a 'Welcome to the family' party. After

dessert, her father invites the two of us
to the 'sombre room'. The invitation,

like the name of the room, is a jolt,
a thunder smack on a clear-sky day.

I see the free-fall in her eyes, but
there's no shake in me. No quake

in me. The couch is plastic covered,
stiff as a never-opened bible.

The question is a thump: *What are
your intentions for our daughter?*

She is 24 and I'm pushing up on 30.
We are toddlers interrogated about

the mess of crumbs defaming
the carpet. I don't avert his eyes,

still suit-sure I'm passing the test
administered by my future father-in-law.

Then the pastor in him shakes the ground
of us with, *You're Jewish.*

Do you know what it means
to be unequally yoked?

We make it two more shaky
years, even through the proclamation
that he couldn't attend, let alone

officiate, his daughter's wedding.
An egg yoke is supposed to
resemble the sun, isn't it?

When You're Not Able to Smile

Time is breaking over
backwards. 29 years

working with young people.
When I was 29 I thought

I would marry Naomi.
At 39, thought it would be

Lisa. Uncle Al at the ready
both times to officiate.

39 years ago another Lisa
hit the stage in a black leotard,

dancing for a talent show
and I learned the sizzle

and burn of lust. Its hissing
whistle, its smoldering

yearn. At 45, I thought
I'd marry Heather.

I cut time in half
in London to move back

to Chicago to make it happen.
It did, but not with me.

45 years ago my family
moved 11 hours from

my family and it tore
a hole inside me as big

as a stopped clock.
11 years ago, sitting

at a table of an Italian
restaurant, my family there

from all over the country
to celebrate my 40th,

and the first Lisa,
(actually, the second)—

the one I thought
I'd marry—soon to be

engaged to someone
else and my Uncle Al,

Alzheimer-ed and
gibberish-ed and

my sister saying,
You've got to smile!

and all the time
I just want to

put my head down
on the table and sob

till the night stops
ticking.

Not Quite

Sometimes I like to tug Mom's black
hair. It's just like the mane
of the pony I'm about to ride.

Her hair's long and shiny and I watch
it from the saddle of the pony
trotting a slow lasso in the dirt.

I'm nervous but it's fun. More so
than the carousel, with its stiff strut.
The kid in front of me says, *Ride 'em*

cowboy! and we both let go of a hand.
I'm sure Mom will yell at me,
for the danger of it, but for now

I'm John Wayne. A few minutes
later I'm hoisted off the pony
and take off towards the black beacon

of Mom. Did she see the John
Wayne of me? The giant grin of me?
I jump into her arms. Her smile—

big, but slightly broken.
She's Mom and not-mom. The same
height and hair, but some other

mom. I start crying and my not-
mom carries me to my own Mom
talking to yet another mom.

(Are there any dads here?) I tug
at my own Mom, who laughs
and hugs my shuddering to a stop.

It's that tugging I never get
quite right, forty-five years later,
no one just quite. If

I pull, they push. No matter if
they drop a, *I like basketball, too.*
You could have invited me.

Then, when I do ask, wanting them
to ride along, there's a *Can't you*
just give me my space? They call

and call until I call back. Push, pull,
tug, tag along, what's the difference?
So many seem exactly what I'm looking for,

and then one night, there's a, *I need*
time alone — please don't call,
a *Maybe we should take a break,*

a *Cancel your ticket to Mexico.* Don't ask
who said what, just know the end
looks identical no matter who starts it.

Grey is More Than a Colour

It steals the black from my beard
and I can't press charges. It's
my grandparents *Grete* and *Hans*
chiseled into the granite cover
to the mausoleum boxes. How they lay

next to each other six grey feet above
ground. It's the stones I lay next to the red
flowers Dad places under their names when
we pay grey respects. It's the grey *why
didn't they want to be buried or ashed*?

It's the overcoat I wear to the cemetery
the grey day we bury Grandma Liz and it's
Shari's grey explanation as to why it's OK
to laugh at the funeral even though
our hearts are heavy with dirt. It's the hollow

grey silence of not tossing back, *It's not OK.*
It's the grey conscience after it's too late
and the grey burn you still feel when
you put it down black on white paper.
It's the air exhaling from the gaping

mouth in the ground before the wooden
box is dropped foot by grey foot into the ditch.
It's our skin when death inhales the bright
out of us. The maggots' teeth. It's our bones
not rattling at being left behind.

Firefly

Firefly light is usually intermittent…. Each blinking pattern is an optical signal that helps fireflies find potential mates. Scientists are not sure how the insects regulate this process to turn their lights on and off. A firefly has an average lifespan of 2 months.
  – The National Geographic website

I'm trying to forget
what if felt like to be aglow,
so I won't notice that I'm not.

That week in Toronto
is an indelible purple stain,
a sizzling smile

that couldn't stop. The incomplete
search for a bison burger. The *it's just
a few blocks* walk to the four miles

away park where we napped in the sun.
The *L* word let loose for the first
time like a firefly from a grape jar.

A week later, when she cries, *I can't
do this*, the L-word boomerangs,
bopping my stunned teeth. My smile's

an imposter, a phantom of buzzing wings.
Six years have creaked by like rusty
quicksand. I hear the tap-tap-tap

of her heels, like a dentist's drill
hitting bone, when she rushes past
my classroom. Occasionally, I'll bump into

her in the hallway in the school
where we still both teach,
her eyes dipped down

seeing what shouldn't have been.
I see the afterglow of lightning
bugs long ago dimmed.

The Search for Meaning

Their bodies, a crooked lecture.
 – Anne Barngrover, from 'Survival Tactics'

You see them in photos —
Iraq, Chile, Mexico,
Auschwitz, Vietnam, Rwanda.
Bodies piled like bloated bricks,
eyes askew, mouths calling
names swallowed in dead air.

When I visit Prague I walk by
a placard about tours to Terezín —
I'd never heard of the place.
I walk out to the other side,
where Terezín turned into Theresienstadt,
where my great-grandmother
was last heard from before she was
stood against a wall and shot or
shipped off to be turned to smoke.
I stand by the wall, a riddle of bullet
holes, and a red hue that's been
washed away but still glows like
a red moon. I try to listen for her
last words, her last thoughts, in this
holding camp, the closest I ever am
to her. I don't speak German, so
it's nothing more than a chant for
my bones to hum. Can you hear it?
What does it mean?

Looking at these crooked
bodies, it's hard to believe
this could ever happen again
with the lesson always
hiding at the bottom of the pile.
Is there anything more
believable than this?

Dropped

What do you do
when water turns gasoline.
Grass is ground glass.
Leaves, lobbed grenades.

Answers, over-
cooked questions. Hard
to swallow. Sticky shreds
stuck in your teeth.

What do you do
when sleep is sandpaper.
Sunrise, Agent Orange.
Hope, a mouth of buckshot.

I'll always love you, now
Who are you?
Always,
a dropped mirror.

Blame

the weather, the waving
sun, the clouds parking
parallel, polluting
blue with the cough of exhaust.
Blame the Rainbo
Club, its photo booth
and the black-and-whites
it took freezing us as a melting
couple. The Silver Cloud,
with its jukebox playing Earth,
Wind and Fire, our cheeks plastered
drunkenly grinding. The Star
Bar—still open, a snap-
shot technicolour. Blame the corner
florist for being open and its
daffodils that died too soon
after I dropped them at her
front door. Blame the Humboldt Pie,
the Polish coffee shop where
she begged to meet to tell me
she wanted to give us a try. Promised
she'd never go back to him.
These dusty place, vacant shells, waving
grave markers. Blame
memory for the crowd it keeps.
For not letting go. Blame
amnesia for never visiting.
Blame time
for slogging in the hour-glass
when you need it light-speed.
Blame God for listening,
for the snap of miracles—

Becky Reagan inviting you
to the ice rink in 4th grade.
Alicia calling from O'Hare instead
of Kenya after serving just six weeks
of a 26-month Peace Corps term.
She came back for you. Two years
later, she packed up and left because
of you. Blame yourself for being you.
For knotting the shoelaces together.
Blame God for no longer granting miracles
three years and counting and counting,
and counting, prayers like popping
balloons. Blame the tide
for always coming in.
Blame the ocean for the waves,
the crash, the calm, the crash,
the get back up.

The Stench of It

Waiting to be brought back for my final radiation session
at Rush Hospital, the TV, as always, is stuck on HGTV
and a pretty couple is tearing up an ugly house in Vegas.
And it stinks. Dog piss so bad it causes mould to sprout

on both sides of the plasterboard. And, of course, I think
of you Mrs. Lancia—un-neighbourly neighbour—the skunk
of you, the rotting tooth of you, the raised hind leg
of you spitting piss all over my Lakinhurst Drive childhood.

And while I lie down and the machine whirs its way
around me, before zooming in to spin its X-ray magic,
(with its sick stench that haunts me when I pee)
into the lump trying to eat its way through me like piss

in snow or through plasterboard, I think of the malignancy
of you, the necrosis of you. Wonder why, like this hungry mass
being radiated for the last time, you chose me.

Barks

Mrs. Gire called me to the board and for the first time
in 2nd grade I got something wrong. She gave me
a strange look like she was happy for me. The night before
I swore I heard barking and the cool side of the pillow
was worthless. Scuttling to school that morning fog-headed,
puffy-headed, I imagined a German Shepherd and me

busting our way down the sidewalk, J.J. Schmidt plinking
himself to the other side of the street, fists hiding
in his pockets at the growl that he didn't even have to hear.
After school, I walked home looking sideways
and backwards for J.J. who must have heard the growl
after all and I swear I heard barks when Grandma

Grete opened the door with a weird smile that wasn't
quite German nor English but seemed to speak in a language
that made me feel what I'd later come to hear my British friends
call *chuffed*. I didn't smell cookies but I still was
chuffed and then there he was licking my face like
it was lapped in chocolate and he seemed smothered

in chocolate marshmallows with his fluffy puppy curls.
Years later when I'm twenty and he's dead I'll sob in
the shower in the hotel in Tel Aviv so my parents can't
hear me though I'm sure they do. And for years after
I still dreamed he was alive and I can still feel the shape
of his skull, how his tail wagged when I massaged his head,

the heavy well of his barks when I'd stop. That's my answer
when students ask me why I don't own a pet even though
I love animals. Watching the lope of my sister's German
Shepherd now that he's hit double-digits, I hear how much
my heart will weep like a shower with the head busted off
when he does too soon what we all get wrong in the end.

What a Teacher's Dream Looks Like

Students won't stop
talking and I know
what I'm saying
is important but
they now have
their headphones in,
and are talking even louder.
And there's a defiance
in the not listening
that's an open-handed
slap. I don't recognise
any of them, but they're
mine. I know they're mine.
And if they're
mine and they won't
listen, what am I
but a hand-print fading
from red to nothing.

A Happy Alzheimer's Poem

Grandpa Hans fell and broke his hip.
He had surgery and for two weeks
he was the happiest I ever saw him.
He was Grandpa, white stubble and all,
but he was dancing with Grandma Grete,
though he hated dancing and Grandma
was dead.

What are you doing, Grandpa?
I just hit a home run.
Where are you?
In Germany, of course.

Grandpa never played baseball
and hadn't been in Germany since he fled
in 1935. He hated everything German.
Grandpa flirted with the nurses
and spoke more in a day than
in the previous six months.
I heard about how he met Grandma
on a donkey ride, how he kicked the winning
goal to defeat France in the World Cup,
how he chopped off his hand at the butcher
shop in São Paulo. I'm sure there was
truth in the giddy telling, even if none
of it was true. Memory, a post-surgery
fun-house mirror.

When Aunt Sheila asks to see my poem
about Uncle Al and I tell her it's too sad,
she tells me, *can you find some not*
sad? I could tell you some things.
He sings notes so loud it rattles our old house

and plays the harmonica like every hole is his friend.
He loves hearing the gurgle of water fountains
and whistles back at the birds.With the right song,
he swings his hips like he's a swaying tree.

> *How are you doing, Uncle Al?*
> *Well, yes, I am.*

> *What's your favorite ice cream?*
> *Uuumm, good.*

People ask, *Why all the sad poems*?
Given all of the sad things to metaphor
over, where's the time for happy?

But maybe Aunt Sheila's got it right—
there's got to be notes of happy
floating on the hip of sad.
And when I tell my students
they need to look at the world
from odd angles, maybe this is it:
Grandpa waltzing with Grandma
in his hospital bed to a song
only he hears. Uncle Al chanting
blessings through the holes of a harmonica.

Gratitude and Acknowledgements

Family: Mom, Dad, Lara, Griffin, Aunt Sheila, Shari, Gayle, Michael and families, Aunt Doris and the Rogelbergs for always supporting and believing in me and to Grandma Liz, Papa Hans, Grandma Grete, Uncle Ernie, Uncle Chuck and Uncle Al for love and inspiration.

Malika's Kitchen: <u>London:</u> Malika Booker & Roger Robinson —nothing I do with poetry would be possible without the two of you. Nick M, Jacob S-L R, Patricia F, Janett P, Esther P, Be M, Sundra L, Nii A P, Denrele O, Dorothea S, Denise S, Jill A & others for being an incredibly supportive community.
<u>Chicago:</u> avery r. y, Ugochi N, Kevin C, Krista F, Tara B, Duriel H, Toni A L and others for helping mold my writing.

MFA: The Fairfield University Creative Writing program, especially Baron W, Bill P and Eugenia K for your expertise and guidance.

Other Mentors: Afaa M W, Terrance H and Mark D for your expertise and inspiration.

Visiting Poets: Roger R, Amaud J J, Tyehimba J, Kwame D, Adrian M, A Van J, Terrance H, Tim S, Franny C, Hanif A, Kyle D, Raymond A, Rachel L, Caleb F & Aisling F for educating and inspiring my students and me.

Spoken Word Educators: The "superstars" —Raymond A, Dean A, Pete B, Cat B, Keith J and Indigo W for believing in me and inspiring me.

The Poetry Foundation: Steve Y, Don S & Ydalmi N for providing so many opportunities.

Oak Park/River Forest High School: Brenda S, Bob M, Steve G, Dan C., Helen G, Sue B, Cindy M, Susan J, Nancy M, Greg J, Joylynn P A, Sully, Christina S, Langston K, David G, Milton M, Adam L, Christian R, Nicha S, Jessica L, Will W, Phil H, Ito O, Jamaal J, Ricky B, Sarah C, Tiffany P, Sierra K, Donorica H, Diamond S, Nova V, Tabitha H, Cailynn S, Grace F, Asia C, Kelly R, LeKeja D, Noelle B, Iman S, Isaiah M, Chris B, Kris M, Natalie R, Hannah S, Dorothy M, Camara B, Tymmarah A, Marlena W, Patrick C, Vann H, Gabe T, Mo S, Hannah G, Savi V, Charity S, Kara J, Leah K, Maggie F, Majesty G, Grace G, Morgan V, Corina R, Jesus G, Nicholas B, Zaire B, Matt M, & current and past members of the English Division & other current and former members of the Spoken Word Club for your support and inspiration.

Other Friends: Ekere T, Patricia S, , Ravi S, The Vance Family, Karla M, Marty C, Dan C, Patrick T, Anna C, Vicky M, Andy S, Bea C, Bismark A, Sue D, Jemilea W, Mona A, Susannah H, Becky S, Lisa M, Ruth H, Sally C, Inua E, Maggie S, Miriam N, Kayo C, Christian F, Deborah S, Anthony J, Fahro M, Yomi S, George S, Tishani D, Kareem P B, Tolu A, Moses B, Blake M, Patience A, John H, Andrew M, Barbara B, Nate M, Jamila W, Eve E, José O, Danez S, Fatimah A, Kathleen R, Kendra D, Caitlin D, Daniel B, CM B, Marty M, Jack P, Ama C, Tracy K S, Greg P, Marilyn N, Willie P, Dorianne L, Christian C, Raych J, Steve J, Naomi J, Pete S, Tim J, Geoff V, Kurt H, Terry E, John P, Mark B, Nancy B, Laura H, Ginger B/Tom P, Avi L, James B/Laura Y, Bernie H, Andrew B, Jim H, Jess S, Jamie S, Suzanne A, Jazmen M, Pete N, Lisa V, Lisa F, Brendan L, Linda/Doug B, Naomi H, Rich Z, Missy H, Dave S, Danielle Z, Jeanne M, Heather R, Ryan D, Carol J, Vicki C, Steve T, Ardene S, Bill A/Bernadine D, Bill G, Dawn T T, Lionel A, Marlene S, Kathryn G, Pete Q, Tim S, Naomi S N, Hannah B & Anne G for your support.

Taylor V for creating the beautiful cover art.

Jane C, Angela H and Nine Arches Press for believing in *Little Kings* and bringing it into the world.

Some of these poems have appeared in the following:
'"Till It's Gone" appears on the Poetry Society (UK) website. 'Little Kings' first appeared in *Make*. 'Tuesday Mornings at Neon Street Center for Youth' first appeared in *Jelly Bucket*. 'Dear Mrs. Gire' first appeared in *X Magazine* (UK). 'An Evening Prayer' first appeared in *Enizagam* 2011. '"Recipe for Me"' first appeared in *Stoneboat*. 'Quit' first appeared in the *Blood Orange Review*. 'Wolf Man of Wicker Park' first appeared in *Lumina*. '"Something About"' first appeared in *Chicago Literati*. 'Independence' first appeared in *Sixfold*. 'Elmer's Glue Girl' first appeared in *The Roanoke Review*. '"Grayed in and Gray"' appears in *The Golden Shovel Anthology: New Poems Honoring Gwendolyn Brooks* (The University of Arkansas Press) and a segment of it appears in *The Chicago Tribune*. 'On Seventeen Years of Teaching' first appeared in *The Bellingham Review*. 'Mrs. Lancia' first appeared in *Flywheel Magazine*. 'Firefly' first appeared in *The Battered Suitcase*. 'Dropped' first appeared in *Pearl*. 'Blame' first appeared in the *Blood Orange Review*.